Living on a Plain

By Joanne Winne

Children's Press
A Division of Grolier Publishing
New York / London / Hong Kong / Sydney
Danbury, Connecticut

Photo Credits: Cover, pp. 5, 7, 9, 11, 13, 15, 17, 19, 21 © National Geographic Image Collection
Contributing Editor: Jennifer Ceaser
Book Design: Nelson Sa

Visit Children's Press on the Internet at:
http://publishing.grolier.com

Library of Congress Cataloging-in-Publication Data

Winne, Joanne.
  Living on a plain / by Joanne Winne.
    p. cm. — (Communities)
  Includes bibliographical references and index.
  Summary: Three children describe what it is like to live on the plains of Mali, Siberia,
and Kansas.
  ISBN 0-516-23304-1 (lib. bdg.) — ISBN 0-516-23504-4 (pbk.)
  1. Plains—Juvenile literature. 2. Grassland people—Juvenile literature. 3. Human
geography—Juvenile literature. [1. Prairies. 2. Human geography. 3. Prairie ecology. 4.
Ecology.] I. Title. II. Series.

GN393.W56 2000
307.7—dc21

                                                                        00-023362

Contents

My name is Manu (**mah**-nu).

The dry **plains** of Mali
(**mah**-lee) are my home.

A plain is land that is **flat**,
with few hills.

5

This is my **village**.

The houses have walls made of rock.

Every roof is made of straw.

7

My mother and I cross the hot, dry plain.

We go to the **well** to get water.

I ride on our donkey as my mother walks.

9

My name is Ivan.

The **icy** plains of Siberia (si-**beer**-ee-ah) are my home.

11

This is my house.

My house is made of wood.

The **thick** walls keep the inside warm.

13

I like to play **hockey** with my friends.

We skate on the **frozen** pond.

15

My name is Sam.

The **grassy** plains of Kansas are my home.

17

This is the **farmhouse** where I live.

There are big trees in the yard.

19

We grow wheat on our farm.

Horses pull the **harvester** over the flat land.

The harvester cuts the wheat and puts it into piles.

21

New Words

farmhouse (**farm**-hows) a house on a farm

flat (**flat**) even; with few hills

frozen (**froh**-zin) water that has turned into ice from the cold

grassy (**gras**-ee) covered with grass

harvester (**har**-ve-ster) a machine used to cut wheat

hockey (**hok**-ee) a game played on ice; players wear skates and carry sticks

icy (**i**-see) covered with ice

plains (**playnz**) flat land with few hills

thick (**thik**) not thin; wide

village (**vil**-ij) a small group of houses

well (**wel**) a deep hole that is made in the ground to get water

To Find Out More

Books
Living on the Plains
by Allan Fowler
Children's Press

Safari
by Caren Barzelay Stelson
The Lerner Publishing Group

Web Sites
CyberSpace Farm
http://www.cyberspaceag.com
Visit a Kansas farm family. Learn about how they grow and harvest crops. Check out the different farm animals. You can even visit a county fair!

Magical Mali
http://www.ontheline.org.uk/schools/magicmali/home.htm
Explore lots of amazing places in Mali. Find out about the land, weather, music, and people.

23

Index

About the Author
Joanne Winne taught fourth grade for nine years and currently writes and edits books for children. She lives in Hoboken, New Jersey.

Reading Consultants
Kris Flynn, Coordinator, Small School District Literacy, The San Diego County Office of Education

Shelly Forys, Certified Reading Recovery Specialist, W.J. Zahnow Elementary School, Waterloo, IL

Peggy McNamara, Professor, Bank Street College of Education, Reading and Literacy Program